GREAT-GRANDFATHER'S NAME   סבא רבה

HEBREW

ENGLISH

GREAT-GRANDMOTHER'S NAME   סבתא רבה

HEBREW

ENGLISH

GREAT-GRANDFATHER'S NAME   סבא רבה

HEBREW

ENGLISH

GREAT-GRANDMOTHER'S NAME   סבתא רבה

HEBREW

ENGLISH

GREAT-GRANDFATHER'S NAME   סבא רבה

HEBREW

ENGLISH

GREAT-GRANDMOTHER'S NAME   סבתא רבה

HEBREW

ENGLISH

GREAT-GRANDFATHER'S NAME   סבא רבה

HEBREW

ENGLISH

GREAT-GRANDMOTHER'S NAME   סבתא רבה

HEBREW

ENGLISH

FAMILY MEMBER NAME

HEBREW

ENGLISH

FAMILY MEMBER NAME

HEBREW

ENGLISH

FAMILY MEMBER NAME

HEBREW

ENGLISH

FAMILY MEMBER NAME

HEBREW

ENGLISH

FAMILY MEMBER NAME

HEBREW

ENGLISH

FAMILY MEMBER NAME

HEBREW

ENGLISH

A Time to Be Born

A Jewish Baby Journal

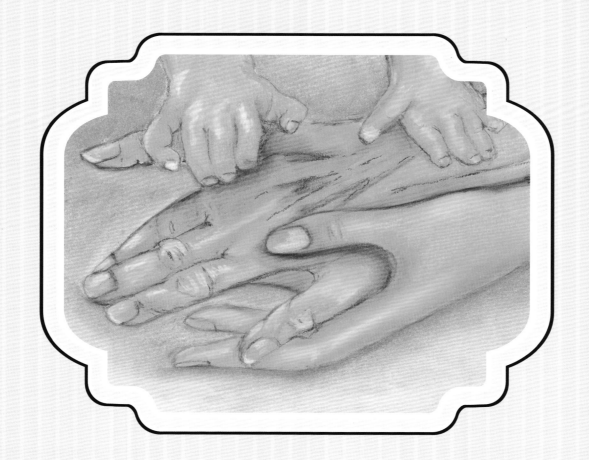

Written and Illustrated by Connie G. Krupin

Written and Illustrated by Connie G. Krupin

Composition and Design by Rikki Campbell Ogden/pixiedesign, llc

To purchase additional copies of this book please visit
www.ATime2BBorn.com

10 9 8 7 6 5 4 3 2 1

Library of Congress Control Number: 2012900184

ISBN: 978-0-615-57127-0

Manufactured in China.

For everything there is a season and a time to every purpose under heaven.
—Ecclesiastes

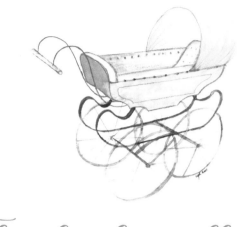

This book is all about

_____

ENGLISH NAME

_____

HEBREW NAME

These precious memories have been lovingly recorded by

_____

May you always know how much you are loved!

For this child I have prayed.
—1 Samuel

Introduction

My dear reader,

Mazal tov and b'sha'a tovah! Best wishes to you and may your baby arrive in good time. Your future is bright and full of possibility.

Let me tell you how this book has found its way to you.

A Time To Be Born; A Jewish Baby Journal began thirty years ago when I became a mother. I was eager to record every moment of our family's new experience with our baby. My husband and I were thrilled to bring our baby into the world and to impart to her the wisdom and beauty of our traditions. Unable to find a baby book that reflected our Jewish family's values, I realized the need to produce my own. As an artist, committed Jew and proud new mother, I was prepared to create.

What I wasn't so prepared for were the sleepless nights, busy days, jobs and everyday life! My babies grew up kind, strong and smart, and began adult lives of their own.

When my own daughter announced that she was to become a mother, I knew that finally, the time had arrived to get out the paints, to research and to write.

The result is now in your hands and ready for your family's story! An heirloom quality art book featuring nearly one hundred original pastel paintings and pages for you to personalize with your own loved ones and memories. I hope that you will find *A Time To Be Born; A Jewish Baby Journal* uplifting and charming, and that you will be inspired to record impressions and memories unique to your baby's life in the warm environment of your Jewish home. There are quotes, traditions and bits of wisdom laced throughout this journal. I hope that these will enlighten you and help you guide and teach.

Remember that one day, this journal will belong to your child. He or she will not only read the words and laugh at the recollections, but will feel the care and love you put into it. Your child is a unique gift to be cherished. This will be your special gift to your child.

My hope is that you and your family members will enjoy recording your precious baby's arrival and unique family history into this journal. As the psalm says, may you live to see the children of your children in happiness and peace.

L'shalom,

Connie Krupin

Connie G. Krupin

Table of Contents

ברוך אתה ה' אלקינו מלך העולם הטוב והמטיב

Blessed are you, God, Ruler of the universe,
the Good and the Doer of good.

A Blessing

May it be the will of our God in Heaven, that He set in your heart the love and awe of Him all your days, so that you do not come to sin.

May your desire be for Torah and the commandments.

May your eyes look straight before you; may your mouth speak wisdom and your heart meditate awe; may your hands be occupied with the commandments and may your feet run to do the will of your Father in Heaven.

Expanded version of the Priestly Blessing
Offered to children prior to Yom Kippur
Adapted by Rabbi Jonathan Z. Maltzman
Kol Shalom, Rockville, MD

There are three partners in the creation of a child; the mother, the father and God.

—Talmud

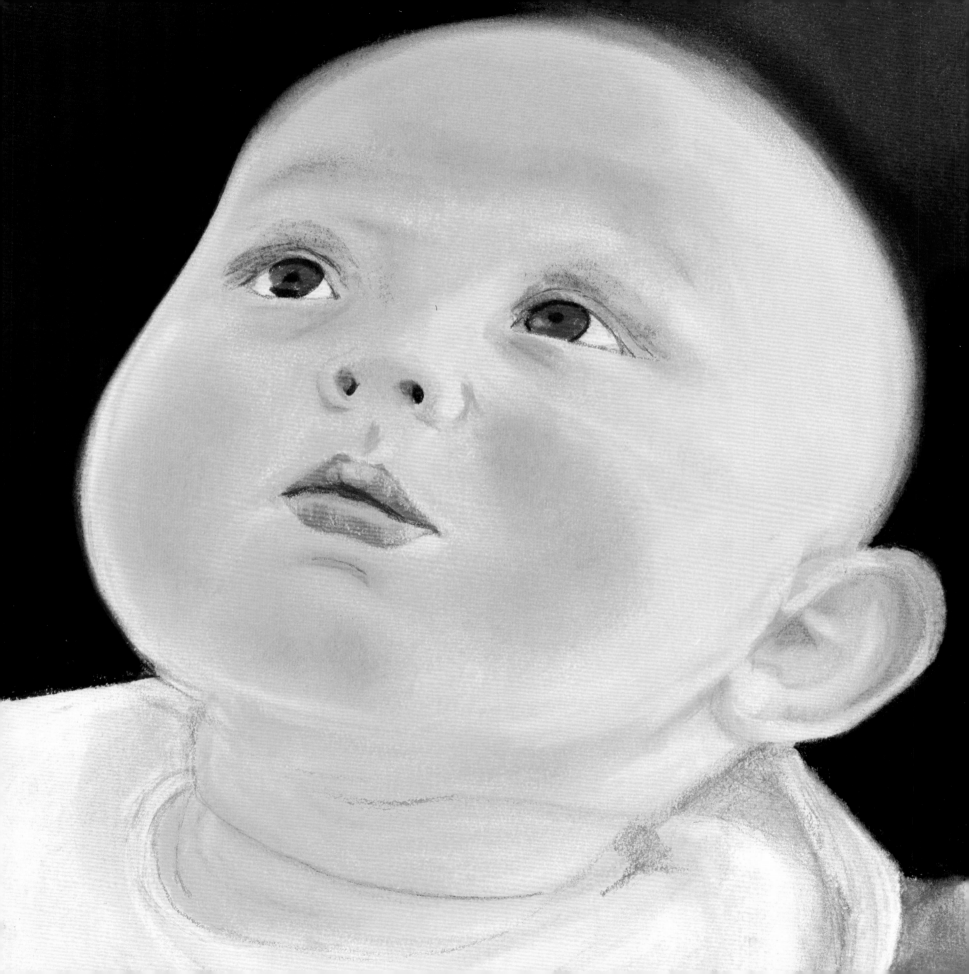

God's Promise

ויוצא אתו החוצה ויאמר הבט נא השמימה וספר הכוכבים אם תוכל לספר אתם ויאמר לו כה יהיה זרע.

And God took him
outside, and said,
"Please look heavenward
and count the stars,
if you are able to
count them."
And God said to him,
"So will be your seed."

—Genesis

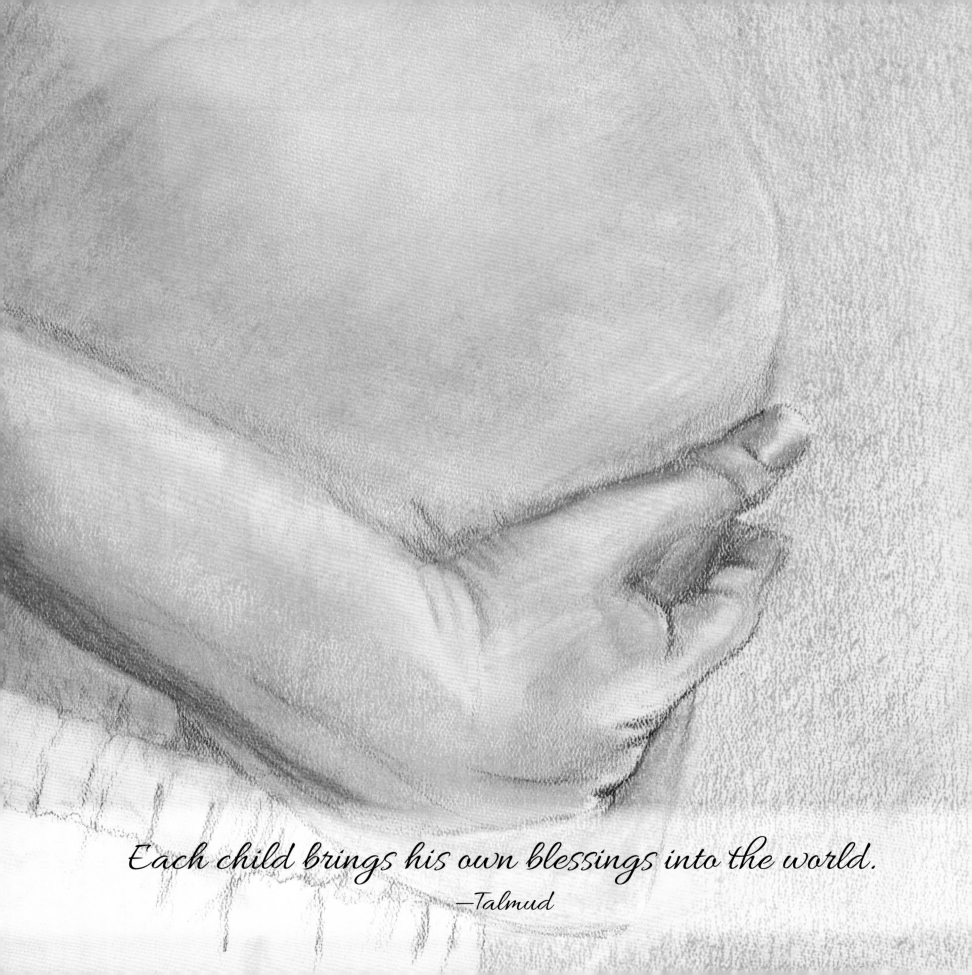

Each child brings his own blessings into the world.

—Talmud

Waiting for Baby

DATE OF FIRST DOCTOR VISIT:

_____

DOCTOR / MIDWIFE'S NAME:

_____

BOOKS PARENTS ARE READING:

_____

_____

_____

CLASSES PARENTS ARE TAKING:

_____

_____

_____

_____

Upon learning about baby...

> Mommy said...

> Daddy said...

> Mommy, I know you want it to be a baby girl, but is it ok if I ask God to make it a puppy?
> —Benny

The mitzvah of being fruitful and multiplying exists so that the earth will be settled. And it is a great mitzvah...because of it, all others exist.

—Sefer HaChinuch, Genesis

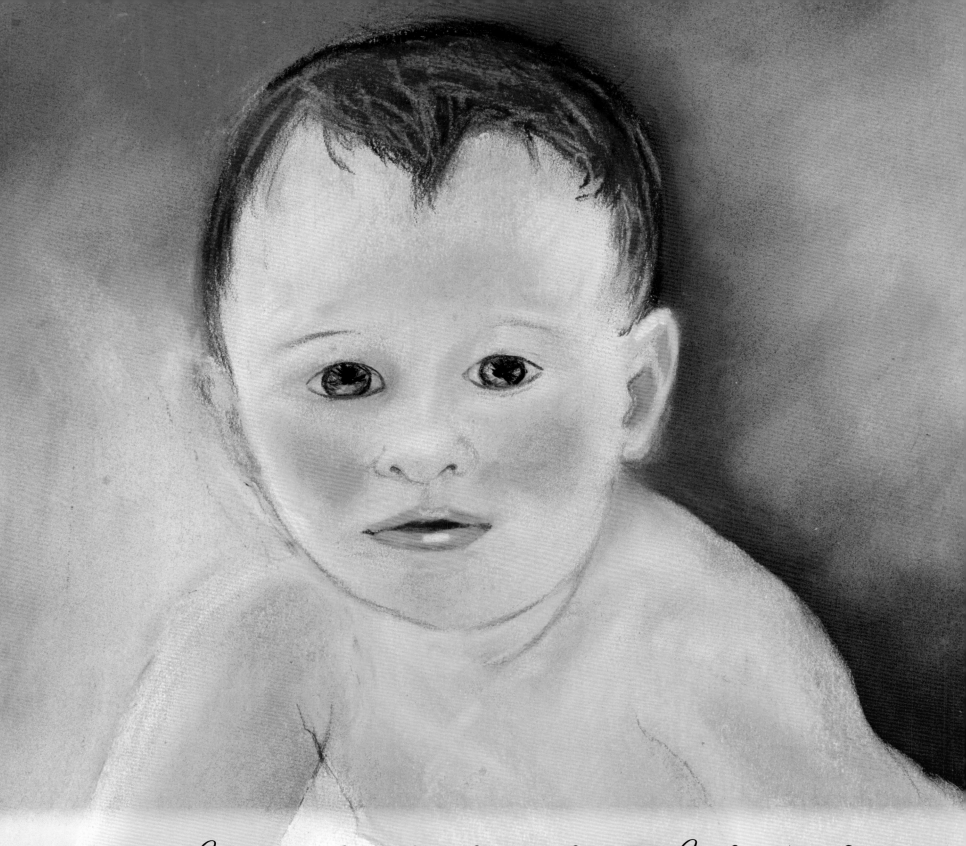

Childbirth lasts only a few hours, but motherhood is forever.

—Anonymous

Labor Diary

LABOR BEGAN AT _____ O-CLOCK __M

ON _____ 20__

WHERE MOTHER WAS WHEN LABOR BEGAN:

_____

FIRST SIGN OF LABOR WAS:

_____

CONTRACTIONS BEGAN AT _____ INTERVALS

AND LASTED FOR _____

DETAILS:

_____

_____

_____

_____

_____

DELIVERY CAME AT _____ O-CLOCK __M

ON _____ 20__

Mother's first words following birth were...

Father's first words following birth were...

God has blessed me with the passion and the power of delivering babies. I am privileged to be part of this true miracle. I see a human life emerge from another human. I experience the parents' overwhelming joy. I can feel God kiss each baby and with that kiss feel the soul awaken.

—Tobie Beckerman, MD OB-GYN Beckerman Women's Health, Bethesda, MD

ברוך אתה ה' אלקינו מלך העולם
שהחיינו וקימנו והגיענו לזמן הזה

Blessed art thou God, Ruler of the Universe, who has kept us in life, sustained us and allowed us to reach this occasion.

Birth Day!

יום הולדת

MONTH OF:

_____

HEBREW MONTH OF:

_____

TIME OF DAY: _____ O-CLOCK __M

DAY:

_____

DAY:

_____

YEAR:

_____

YEAR:

_____

Sunday	**YOM RISHON**
Monday	**YOM SHENI**
Tuesday	**YOM SHLISHI**
Wednesday	**YOM RIVII**
Thursday	**YOM HAMISHI**
Friday	**YOM SHISHI**
Saturday	**YOM SHABBAT**

"What is a birthday? It is a day when the Creator of all life decided the world would be a better place with you in it. And since that day, God has breathed life into you thousands of times a day, giving you many opportunities to make the world brighter with everything you do. So remember on this day, and every day, that who you are is God's gift to you, and who you become is your gift to God."

—Rabbi Levi Shemtov
Director, American Friends of Lubavitch
Washington, DC

מי שגמלך טוב הוא יגמלך כל טוב סלה

May the one who has granted you all kindness,
always grant you kindness, selah.

Shayna Punim

LENGTH AT BIRTH:

WEIGHT AT BIRTH:

APGAR SCORE AT BIRTH:　　　**2ND:**

BLOOD TYPE:

CIRCUMFERENCE OF HEAD:

EYE COLOR:　　　　　**LATER:**

HAIR COLOR:　　　　　**LATER:**

BABY MOST RESEMBLES:

BABY'S HANDPRINT　　　　　　　　　　BABY'S FOOTPRINT

Just as my parents have planted for me,
so I plant for my children.
—Talmud

A Time to Plant

Trees stand at the center of Jewish symbolism.
Even with regard to the Torah, it is said,
"She is a tree of life for those who grasp her,
and all who hold onto her are happy."

In ancient times, it was customary upon the birth of a child to plant a tree in his honor; a cedar for a boy and a cypress or other evergreen for a girl. This custom appears in the Babylonian Talmud.

When the child was to be married, branches from the tree were intertwined to form the four poles of the chuppah, or wedding canopy.

This beautiful and symbolic custom is rarely practiced today. A contemporary tradition is to plant a tree in Israel in honor of a child's birth.

The life of a tree exceeds the life on an individual. Therefore, the practical and symbolic act of planting ensures that one generation preserves and provides for the next.

In the story of Adam and Eve, the tree is seen as a metaphor for individual choice.

A Snapshot in Time

NEWS OF THE DAY

POPULAR MUSIC

PRESIDENT

COST OF THE
AVERAGE HOME

COST OF A GALLON
OF MILK

COST OF AN HOUR
OF BABYSITTING

23

Brothers and Sisters

I HAVE _____ BROTHERS   **I HAVE _____ SISTERS**

THEIR NAMES ARE:

_____

_____

_____

_____

_____

THEIR BIRTHDAYS ARE:

_____

_____

_____

_____

A happy heart gives life to a person.
Joyfulness lengthens one's days.

—Talmud

"A mother's love is like a flame. No matter how many additional fires are lit from it, the original flame is not diminished. Like God's love for all His children, a mother's love is boundless yet individual; constantly providing warmth, support, attention and care."
—Nechama D. Shemtov, AURA Jewish Women, Washington, D.C.

In Mother's Words

Values that are most important to me...

The best thing about being a mother is...

My favorite memory of my father is...

My favorite memory of my mother is...

MY NAME IS:

_____

I MOST RESEMBLE:

_____

THE PERSON I MOST ADMIRE:

_____

BECAUSE:

_____

_____

_____

My favorite childhood memory is...

My proudest accomplishment is...

As a child, I wanted to grow up to be...

The neighborhood I grew up in was...

Did my parents pray for me?
I am their prayers answered.
Therefore, I am a miracle!

In Father's Words

Values that are most important to me...

The best thing about being a father is...

As a child, I wanted to grow up to be...

My favorite memory of my mother is...

MY NAME IS:

_____

I MOST RESEMBLE:

_____

THE PERSON I MOST ADMIRE:

_____

BECAUSE:

_____

_____

_____

My favorite childhood memory is...

My proudest accomplishment is...

My favorite memory of my father is...

The neighborhood I grew up in was...

Many women have done excellently,
but you have exceeded them all.
—Proverbs

Grandmother's Memories

NAME

_____

CHILD'S NAME FOR HER

_____

HER FAVORITE THING TO DO WHEN SHE WAS A GIRL

_____

HER FAVORITE SUBJECT IN SCHOOL

_____

A BIG INFLUENCE IN HER LIFE

_____

THE BEST THING THAT EVER HAPPENED TO HER

_____

HER PROUDEST ACCOMPLISHMENT

_____

SPECIAL MEMORIES

_____

_____

NAME

_____

CHILD'S NAME FOR HER

_____

HER FAVORITE THING TO DO WHEN SHE WAS A GIRL

_____

HER FAVORITE SUBJECT IN SCHOOL

_____

A BIG INFLUENCE IN HER LIFE

_____

THE BEST THING THAT EVER HAPPENED TO HER

_____

HER PROUDEST ACCOMPLISHMENT

_____

SPECIAL MEMORIES

_____

_____

My mother was driving with my 5 year old son, Jake, who was just learning to read. Excited about his new skill, he read every word he saw pass by on signs and buildings. From the backseat, Mom heard "stop...no turns...pizza...." Suddenly, Jake said, "yamaka!" Mom asked, "Where does it say yamaka?" Jake pointed out a building. Mom looked...and there on the building were the letters YMCA.

—Suzy, Jake's Mom

The simplest toy, one that even the youngest child can operate, is called a grandparent.
—Sam Levinson

Grandfather's Memories

NAME	**NAME**
CHILD'S NAME FOR HIM	**CHILD'S NAME FOR HIM**
HIS FAVORITE THING TO DO WHEN HE WAS A BOY	**HIS FAVORITE THING TO DO WHEN HE WAS A BOY**
HIS FAVORITE SUBJECT IN SCHOOL	**HIS FAVORITE SUBJECT IN SCHOOL**
A BIG INFLUENCE IN HIS LIFE	**A BIG INFLUENCE IN HIS LIFE**
THE BEST THING THAT EVER HAPPENED TO HIM	**THE BEST THING THAT EVER HAPPENED TO HIM**
HIS PROUDEST ACCOMPLISHMENT	**HIS PROUDEST ACCOMPLISHMENT**
SPECIAL MEMORIES	**SPECIAL MEMORIES**

Zaidy, since God made Moses live for 120 years, can you ask Him to do that for you, too?

—Evan

Like All Jewish Mothers

Like all Jewish mothers, I do not need Spock
To help with the kids that I raise.
I do not need Bettelheim, don't need Gesell
I just give 'em love and give plenty of praise
Like all Jewish mothers!

I give my kids culture before they are three.
The lessons in ballet begin.
And though I may nag, I make sure that they play
The cello, piano or else violin!

Like all Jewish mothers, I'm strict with my kids.
I never will spoil them and yet
I give them a car and a phone of their own,
A color TV and a stereo set
Like all Jewish mothers!

Some say I'm loaded with guilt!
Use guilt with my children up to the hilt!
Some say I'm pushy as well.
A push sometimes helps; you never can tell!

Just take Jerome Kern
And add Isaac Stern you'll agree!
And add Edward Teller!
Include Joseph Heller,
Jan Pierce, Sills and Gershwin, all three!
They ALL had mothers like me!

Circa 1968
by Edie Katz (1920–2009)

It is not the place
that honors its man,
but the man that
honors his place.
—Talmud

Welcome Home!

BRIT YITZCHAK

ברית יצחק

(Sephardic tradition): is held on the evening preceding the newborn's Brit Milah. The baby's father reads the final paragraph regarding his obligation to circumcise his son. Shulchan Aruch

ADDRESS

_____

_____

_____

SHALOM ZACHOR

שלום זכר

(Ashkenazi tradition): (Literally; Farewell to memory) Ashkenazi tradition holds that on the first Friday night following the birth of a boy, a joyous gathering is held. The Talmud teaches that while the baby developed in the womb, he was taught the entire Torah, but upon birth, an angel struck him on his mouth, causing him to forget. As he will now have to relearn his entire life, we "console" him.

ZEVED HABAT

זבד הבת

Gift of the Daughter is a ceremony dating from the 17th Century and is drawn from the utterance of Jacob's wife Leah, following the birth of her son, Zevulun. Leah said, "Zevadani Elokim oti Zeved Tov," "God has granted me a gift." (Genesis) This primarily Sephardic custom is performed at home or at the synagogue. Special melodies and verses from the Song of Songs are traditionally sung.

God brought them to Adam to see what Adam would call them; and whatever Adam called each living creature would be its name.

—Genesis

Baby is Given a Name

HEBREW:

_____

ENGLISH:

_____

BABY IS NAMED FOR:

_____

RELATIONSHIP:

_____

QUALITIES OF THIS PERSON(S) TO EMULATE:

_____

_____

_____

Jewish tradition holds that the name given to a child is of great importance as it relates to the essence of an individual. Consider that HASHEM, literally meaning "the name," is a common reference to God. In fact, there are many names for God, each referring to God's many attributes.

A Parent's Prayer

My son is my prayer
Unto You God.

For he is a sign of the covenant
And he is the continuance of the sign.

He is my offering
Of faith
In the world, in You, and in man.

He is so tender and sweet,
So loving and kind
With qualities so deep.

So watch over him when we cannot,
And be with him when we are not.
For he is our prayer unto You.

Rabbi Stuart Weinblatt
Congregation B'nai Tzedek
Potomac, Maryland

Every male among you shall be circumcised...
And that shall be a sign of the covenant between ME and You.

—Genesis

Brit Milah

Mommy, when are the people coming for Sammy's brisket?
—Aaron

MOHEL'S NAME:

_____

DATE OF CEREMONY:

_____

PLACE:

_____

SITTING SANDEK:

_____

STANDING SANDEK:

_____

KVATTER (GODFATHER):

_____

KVATTERIN (GODMOTHER):

_____

WHO ATTENDED:

_____

_____

_____

Tradition tells us that by design God left the process of creation unfinished, thereby requiring mankind to complete the work. By circumcising our sons, we are fulfilling the mitzvah. The child is brought into the covenant and the process of creation continues.

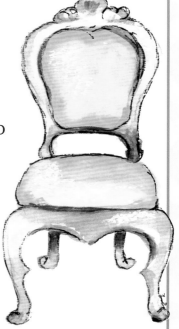

The prophet, Elijah is said to have railed against the behavior of his day which he saw as betraying God's law. At one point, Elijah complained to God that Jewish behavior is so bad that in years to come, all of God's commandments will be forgotten and not one mitzvah will be practiced.

God responded that Elijah was mistaken; that the mitzvah of Brit Milah (circumcision) will be practiced for all time. Elijah is commanded to be present at EVERY Brit ceremony to personally witness the fulfillment of the mitzvah. A special chair is provided for his visit.

A good name is better than precious oil.
—Ecclesiastes

Simchat Bat

DATE OF CEREMONY:

_____

PLACE:

_____

WHO ATTENDED:

_____

_____

_____

_____

_____

_____

Ashkenazi Jews (of Eastern European descent) traditionally name a baby for a deceased relative so that the name continues. Sephardic Jews (of Spanish descent) name the baby after a living relative. The baby is said to inherit the essential qualities of the name.

In ancient times and throughout the middle ages, welcoming baby girls was done in an intimate, all female setting. During the middle ages, candies were given to all the young girls present. They would dance around the cradle and shout, "What will the the baby's name be?" The mother would respond by announcing the baby's name. The cradle would then be lifted as a gesture of validation.

In the 20th Century and to the present, the naming of a girl commonly takes place in the synagogue, often on the Shabbat morning service following the child's birth. An aliyah (call to the Torah) is given and a "mi sheberach" prayer for the mother, father and baby is offered. A kiddush in the baby's honor customarily follows.

For every first born among the Israelites..is Mine..
—Numbers

Pidyon Ha Ben

Ceremony of the Redemption of the Son

DATE OF CEREMONY:

_____

PLACE:

_____

OFFICIANT:

_____

The first and best of all things belong to God. While the majority of the Children of Israel committed the sin of the Golden Calf, the Levites did not, and God chose the tribe of Levi over the firstborn son for service in the Temple. However, even though their place has been taken by the Levites, the firstborn still retain a certain degree of sanctity, and for this reason, traditionally, they are redeemed. In biblical times, this was done by paying to a Kohen (Priest) a small sum five silver shekels. Today, usually five silver dollars is offered. This beautiful ceremony takes place following the 30th day of birth. _Note that if the mother is a Bat-Cohen or a Bat-Levi, the ceremony is not performed._

There are many details surrounding this custom in Jewish tradition. For details relating to one's own ceremony, it is best to check with your Rabbi!

There are two ways to live your life. One is as though nothing is a miracle. The other is as though everything is a miracle.
—Albert Einstein

Weight and Length

DOCTOR: _____

DOCTOR'S COMMENTS:

_____

_____

_____

DATE OF FIRST VISIT: _____

WEIGHT: _____

LENGTH: _____

AGE	DATE	WEIGHT	LENGTH	COMMENTS
1 month				
2 months				
3 months				
4 months				
5 months				
6 months				
8 months				
1 year				
18 months				
2 years				
30 months				
3 years				
4 years				
5 years				

Nechama's Chicken Soup

whole chicken, cut up
3 carrots
2 celery stalks
1 onion, chopped
2 parsnips
2 zucchini
2 yellow squash
1 sweet potato

Place chicken parts in a large pot. Add enough water to cover. Add vegetables and bring to a boil.

Skim off fat. Cook over low heat for two hours or more. You may then add noodles and cook for 5 minutes more.

Serve with love!

Immunizations

IMMUNIZATION RECORD FOR:

_____

AGE	HEP B	ROTO-VIRUS	DPT	HEM. INFLU	PNEU-MONIA	INACT. POLIO	INFLU-ENZA	MMR	VARI-CELLA	HEP A	MENIN
1 month											
2 months											
3 months											
4 months											
5 months											
6 months											
8 months											
1 year											
18 months											
2 years											
30 months											
3 years											
4 years											
5 years											

Baby's Firsts

ACTIVITY	DATE	AGE
Raises head alone and holds it up		
Kicks vigorously & tries to turn		
Rolls from back to tummy		
First social smile		
First laugh		
Makes known likes		
Makes known dislikes		
Recognizes mother & father		
Discovers hands & feet		
Discovers own voice, coos & babbles		
Imitates sounds & motions		
Sleeps through the night		
Reaches for & Holds objects		
Sits without support		

ACTIVITY	DATE	AGE
Crawls		
Stands with help		
Stands alone		
Plays "peek a boo"		
Holds cup & drinks		
Holds spoon		
Pulls self up & stands alone		
First Steps		
Helps in dressing self		
Identifies colors		
Counts to five		
Turns pages of a book		
Pedals a tricycle		
Catches a ball		

Baby's Teeth

DENTIST'S NAME:

_____

MY FIRST TOOTH ARRIVED ON:

_____

DATE OF FIRST VISIT:

_____

POSITION:

_____

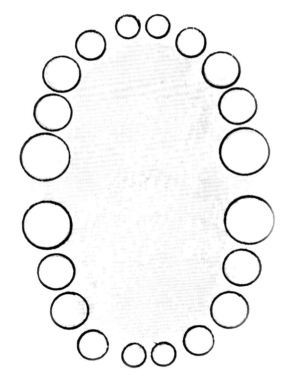

TOOTH	AVG. AGE	DATE OF ERUPTION
A. Central Incisor	6–12 months	
B. Lateral Incisor	9–16 months	
C. Canine	16–23 months	
D. 1st Molar	13–19 months	
E. 2nd Molar	23–33 months	

How will I teach my child? I will teach by what I do and what I say. I will speak my values clearly and unequivocally. I will speak with love and respect. I will speak of my values often. Over and over and over again until I become a voice inside my child.

Development of Character

PLAYS WITH OTHER CHILDREN (AT AGE _____):

_____

RESPONDS TO OTHERS:

_____

IS ENTHUSIASTIC/RETICENT:

_____

RESPONDS TO PETS (AT AGE _____):

_____

COMMENTS:

_____

_____

The Talmud says: The name of the angel in charge of conception is Night; he takes each drop and places it before the Holy One, saying to Him, "Master of the Universe, what is this drop to become; a strong man or a weak man, a wise man or a fool, a rich man or a poor man?"

But he does not say, "A righteous man or a wicked man." The Rabbis added, "Everything is in the hands of Heaven except the fear of Heaven."

—Talmud

How wonderful it is that nobody need wait a single moment before starting to improve the world! —Anne Frank

Playtime

FAVORITE GAMES:

_____

FAVORITE TOY:

_____

FAVORITE TYPES OF PLAY:

_____

FAVORITE STORIES & RHYMES:

_____

_____

FAVORITE SONGS:

_____

YIDDISH RHYMES:

Potchy Potchy Kichelakh!
Tateh koyfen shichelakh!
Mama shtriken zechelakh!
A guzunt in dayneh pekelakh!

Clap, Clap your hands (cookies)!
Daddy's buying you shoes!
Mommy's knitting you socks!
Good health to you!

Hundosh, Hydosh, Pitzelah,
Madeleh (girl) / Yingeleh (boy)

Rock back & forth
Little girl / boy

When a child laughs,
the heavens rejoice!

Bedtime

BABY'S SLEEP PATTERN:

_____

_____

FAVORITE BEDTIME STORY (AT AGE ____):

_____

FAVORITE BEDTIME SONG (AT AGE ____):

_____

PARENTS' COMMENTS:

_____

_____

_____

BABY'S BEDTIME RITUALS:

_____

_____

Parents have been reciting the Shema prayer to their babies and children for millenia. This prayer is the cornerstone of the Jewish faith, affirming our belief in one God. Traditionally, the first of 3 paragraphs is recited or sung.

A touching story recalls Rabbi Eliezer Silver from the United States arriving in 1945 at a Catholic orphanage in Alsace-Lorraine in search of Jewish children who had been hidden there during the war. In response to the rabbi's request to reclaim the children, the priest replied that there were no Jewish children residing at the orphanage. The rabbi replied, "May I be allowed to return at bedtime to see the children?" The rabbi's request was granted. He stood before the children and simply began singing the Shema. Upon hearing the beautiful prayer, the Jewish children's eyes widened and they cried, "Mama!" "Maman!" "Mamushka!"—each in his own language. The rabbi then said to the priest, "These are my children. I will take them home with me."

Rozinkes mit Mandlen

Raisins with Almonds

In dem beys hamikdosh in a vinkl cheyder
zitst di almona bas Tzion aleyn
Ir ben yochidl Yideleh
Vigt sie k'seder
Un zingt im tsum shlofen a leidele sheyn

In a corner of the synagogue
sits a widow; daughter of Zion.
her only son, Judah
she rocks continuously
and sings him to sleep—a sweet lullaby:

Ay-lu-lu-lu-lu

Unter Ydeleh's vigele
Shteyt a klor vays tzigele
Dos tzigele is geforn handlen
Dos vet zayn dayn baruf
Rosinkes un mandlen

Under Judah's cradle
Stands a pure white goat.
The goat went to wander.
That is our fate.
Raisins and Almonds

Shlof-zhe, Yidele, Shlof
Shlof-zhe, Yidele, Shlof

Sleep, Judah, sleep
Sleep, Judah, sleep

This popular Yiddish lullaby by Abraham Goldfaden (1840-1906) comforted Jewish babies throughout European Jewish communities in the 19th and 20th centuries. Many Bubbies and Zaidies remember it fondly to this day. One dear Bubbie has now passed it on to you!

A mother understands
what a child does not say.
—Jewish Proverb

Baby Talk

FIRST MEANINGFUL SOUNDS (AT AGE _____):

_____

FIRST WORD (AT AGE _____):

_____

REPEATS A WORD (AT AGE _____):

_____

FAVORITE WORD:

_____

PUTS 2 WORDS TOGETHER (AT AGE _____):

_____

FIRST SENTENCE (AT AGE _____):

_____

REPEATS A SONG (AT AGE _____):

_____

REPEATS A PRAYER (AT AGE _____):

_____

WORD LIST: **AGE:**

_____

_____

_____

_____

_____

_____

_____

_____

MEMORABLE PHRASES AND SENTENCES:

_____

_____

_____

_____

_____

_____

_____

_____

A child speaks in the marketplace the way he heard
his parents speak at home. —Babylonian Talmud

The man whose good deeds exceed his wisdom
is like a tree with few branches and many roots:
all the raging winds will not move him.

—Pirke Avot

First Haircut

NAME:

DATE:

AGE:

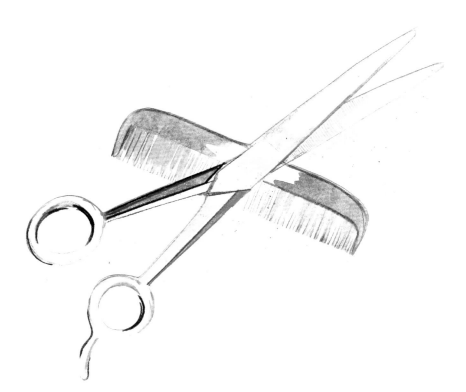

LOCK OF HAIR

Tradition says that upon a boy reaching the age of three a ceremony known as an Upsherin is performed wherein the child's receives his first haircut. This lovely custom relates to God's commandment that the first yields of a tree may not be harvested until after the third year. The Rabbis explain that this gives the tree time to form a firm foundation.

Challah

4 pkg yeast
1 cup warm water
2/3 cup + 1 tsp sugar
3 cups boiling water
1 cup canola oil
2/3 cup honey
2 tbsps salt
2 cup raisins (optional)
15 cups flour
8 eggs (at room temperature)

Dissolve yeast in warm water and 1 tsp of sugar.

Combine in medium sized bowl: boiling water, canola oil, 2/3 cup sugar, honey, salt, and raisins (if using)

Refrigerate to cool until warm. While it cools, measure and sift flour into a large bowl.

Add yeast to refrigerated mixture Add 6 eggs and 2 egg whites, one at a time. Save yolks.

Add flour and knead. Keep adding flour until barely sticky. Add more flour if necessary.

Brush oil on top and cover with a cloth. Set into a warm (not hot) oven.

Let rise for 1 hour. Take out and knead. Divide into four portions.* Form into loaves and braid.

Place on ungreased cookie sheet and let rise for 45 minutes.

Brush with yolk. Bake at 350° for 45 minutes. Yields 4 challot.

*This is the point at which an egg sized portion of challah is separated, recalling Temple times and the following blessing is recited:

ברוך אתה ה' אלקינו מלך העולם אשר קדשנו במצותיו וצונו להפריש חלה

Blessed are You, our God, Ruler of the Universe, Who has sanctified us with Your Commandments and commanded us to separate challah.

Shabbat

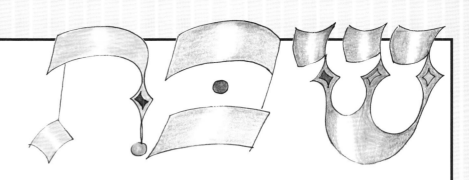

PRESENT AT BABY'S FIRST SHABBAT WERE (AT AGE _____):

_____

_____

WHERE WE WELCOMED SHABBAT:

_____

FIRST TASTE OF CHALLAH:

_____

FAVORITE THING ABOUT SHABBAT:

_____

_____

PARENTS' BLESSING:
May the Lord bless you and keep you.
May the Lord show you favor and be gracious to you.
May the Lord show you kindness and grant you peace.

ישמך אלקים כשרה רבקה רחל ולאה

May you be like Sarah, Rebecca, Rachel and Leah.

ישמך אלקים כאפרים וכמנשה

May you be like Ephraim and Menashe.

Shabbat Candlelighting

ברוך אתה ה' אלקינו
מלך העולם אשר קדשנו
במצותיו וצונו להדליק נר
של שבת

*Blessed are you, God,
Ruler of the universe who
commands us to light the
Shabbat candles.*

Tradition holds that upon reaching the age of three, the age at which a child can grasp an understanding of Jewish learning, girls learn the prayers and begin lighting one candle on Shabbat. The custom of young girls lighting Shabbat candles appears in the text "Aruch HaShulchan."

Today, it is customary for married women to light at least two candles on Erev Shabbat. Many light a candle for each family member.

The midrash explains that Abraham's wife, Sarah, lit a lamp every Friday evening to honor the Divine day of rest. This lamp miraculously burned all week until the next Friday evening. However, when Sarah died, the light was extinguished.

On the day of Sarah's passing, Rebecca was born. When she was brought to Sarah's tent as Isaac's intended wife, the miracle of the lamp returned, thus bringing with it the radiance of Shabbat holiness.

The shofar is a wake up call from God!
—Rachel

The High Holidays

Rosh Hashana and Yom Kippur

HOW AND WHERE FIRST ROSH HASHANA WAS OBSERVED (AT AGE _____):

_____

_____

WHO CELEBRATED WITH US:

_____

_____

BABY'S REACTION TO HEARING THE SHOFAR BLASTS:

_____

FAVORITE HOLIDAY FOOD:

_____

Rosh Hashana begins on the 1st day of Tishrei and lasts for two days. This date is written in the Torah and together with Yom Kippur, which occurs ten days later, the holidays are known as the "Days of Awe." We prepare ourselves for the days of awe during the previous month of Elul, during which, it is said that God's presence is felt especially closely.

Foods symbolizing hopes for the coming year are customarily eaten. Apples dipped in honey symbolize a sweet year ahead. The Pomegranate with its 613 seeds, represents good deeds and mitzvot (commandments). Sephardic tradition includes a Passover style seder incorporating these and other foods!

71

The significance of "gelt" (money) on Chanukah is to signify a free people as the Jews became after the victorious rebellion led by Judah Macabee. While under Syrian Greek rule, coins of the realm were stamped "Judea Capta" (Judea is conquered).Only an autonomous people can mint its own coins.

Potato Latkes

Canola oil for frying

3 large potatoes (peeled, quartered)

2 small onions (peeled, quartered)

1 lemon

2 large eggs

3/4 teaspoon salt

1/2 teaspoon baking powder

2 tablespoons flour

pepper

Over low to medium heat, cover the bottom of a frying pan with 1/4 inch of oil.

Place half of the potatoes and half the onions into the bowl of a food processor fitted with a metal blade. Squeeze in a few drops of lemon juice. Process until the chunks are small, no larger than 1/2 inch. (Do not puree.) Transfer to a large bowl. Repeat with remaining potatoes and onions.

Add eggs, salt, baking powder, flour, pepper, and a few more drops of lemon juice, to the potato and onion mixture. Mix well.

Turn the heat under the oil to medium high. To test the heat, put a tiny amount of potato batter into the oil—if it sizzles, the oil is hot enough.

Use a soup spoon to scoop up the batter and carefully pour into the pan. Leaving room between the latkes to use a spatula in the pan to flip them. When one side is golden-brown, turn over and fry the opposite side until golden.

If the latkes are cooking very quickly or starting to burn, turn down the heat a little. Add more oil if it starts to disappear after a few batches. If the batter at the bottom of the bowl is a little watery, mix in 1 teaspoon flour. Yields 20 latkes.

TIP: Drain latkes on the inside of large supermarket paper bags—they absorb the oil very well.

Recipe courtesy of Paula Shoyer, "The Kosher Baker"

Chanukah

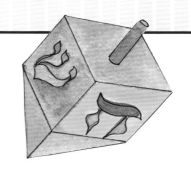

MEMORIES OF FIRST CHANUKAH (AT AGE _____):

_____

_____

WHO CELEBRATED WITH US:

_____

_____

FAVORITE GIFTS AND GELT:

_____

FAVORITE THINGS ABOUT CHANUKAH:

_____

LIGHTING THE CHANUKIAH (MENORAH):

Candles are placed in the chanukiah from right to left; one for each night plus the shammash candle (helper). The shammash is lit first and is used to light the others. One candle is added every night for eight nights. The candle representing the newest night (to the left) is lit first and is followed by its neighbor to the right and so on. Follow by reciting the prayers:

ברוך אתה ה' אלקינו מלך העולם אשר קדשנו במצותיו וצונו להדליק נר של חנכה

Blessed are You, our God, Ruler of the Universe, who sanctifies us with Your commandments and commands us to light the Chanukah candles.

ברוך אתה ה' אלקינו מלך העולם שעשה נסים לאבותינו בימים ההם בזמן הזה

Blessed are You, our God, Ruler of the Universe, who performed miracles for our anscestors in those days at this time.

For the first night only, add:

ברוך אתה ה' אלקינו מלך העולם שהחינו וקימנו והגיענו לזמן הזה

Blessed are You, our God, Ruler of the Universe, who has kept us in life, sustained us, and has allowed us to reach this occasion.

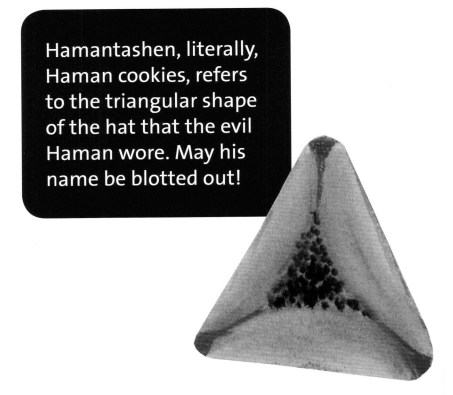

Hamantashen, literally, Haman cookies, refers to the triangular shape of the hat that the evil Haman wore. May his name be blotted out!

Bubbie's Favorite Hamantashen

FOR THE DOUGH:

3 eggs

1 cup oil

1 cup sugar

1 cup baking powder

1/2 cup water

1/2 cup orange juice

1/8 tsp salt

4 cups flour (you may need an extra cup or two)

FOR THE FILLING:

Prune jam or fruit pie filling of your choosing: cherry, apple, lemon, poppyseed, apricot

Combine ingredients in order listed to make a soft dough that is not sticky. Let stand for fifteen minutes.

Divide into four parts.

Roll to 1/4" thickness on a floured board.

Cut into 4" circles. Place a spoonful of filling in the center of each circle.

Lift the sides of the triangle into the center to form a "triangle pocket."

Brush the top with beaten egg yolk.

Place on baking sheet and bake at 30 minutes at 350 degrees until brown.

Ess, kinderlakh, ess! Eat, children, eat!

Purim

FIRST TIME LISTENING TO THE READING OF MEGILLAT ESTHER:

_____

REACTION TO THE LOUD GROGGER:

_____

FIRST PURIM COSTUME:

_____

FIRST GIVING AND RECEIVING OF SHALACH MANOT (GIFT BASKET OF GOODIES):

_____

FIRST TASTE OF HAMANTASHEN:

_____

On Purim, we read the biblical story of Queen Esther, whose bravery saved the Jewish People from the hand of the wicked Haman. The four mitzvot associated with the joyous holiday are: witnessing of the reading of the megillah (story), giving gifts of food, giving charity and feasting merrily!

As God's miracles were made possible through the actions of Queen Esther & Mordechai, it is said that God's presence was "masked," thus the custom of wearing costumes!

75

CELEBRATIONS AND HOLIDAYS

Passover

פסח

HOW AND WHERE FIRST SEDER WAS OBSERVED (AT AGE _____):

_____

_____

WHO CELEBRATED WITH US:

_____

_____

_____

FIRST TIME FINDING THE AFIKOMEN:

_____

REWARD FOR FINDING THE AFIKOMEN:

_____

FIRST TIME ASKING THE FOUR QUESTIONS:

_____

FAVORITE HOLIDAY FOODS:

_____

FAVORITE HOLIDAY SONGS:

_____

Why do we spill a drop of wine as we name each plague? Because even though it was our enemies on whom God's wrath was inflicted, we show compassion for the suffering of others by lessening our own joy.

Grandma, why do you only speak English?
—Tifarah *(lives in Israel and speaks Hebrew and English)*

Yom Ha'atzmaut

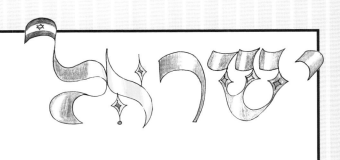

Israel Independence Day

HOW AND WHERE FIRST YOM HA'ATZMANT WAS OBSERVED (AT AGE ____):

_____

_____

Hatikvah—"The Hope"
Israeli National Anthem

Kol od balevav P'nimah Nefesh Yehudi homiyah	As long as the Jewish spirit is yearning deep in the heart,
Ulfa'atey mizrach kadima Ayin l'tzion tzofiyah.	With eyes turned toward the East, looking toward Zion,
Od lo avdah tikvatenu Hatikvah bat shnot alpayim	Then our hope—the two-thousand- year-old hope—will not be lost:
L'hiyot am chofshi b'artzenu Eretz Tzion v'Yerushalayim.	To be a free people in our land, The land of Zion and Jerusalem.

MAY 14, 1948 / IYYAR 5 5708

On this date, Israel's Declaration of Independence was read
and signed in Tel Aviv. The Jewish homeland was born!

First Friends

NAME:

_____

_____

_____

_____

AGE:

_____

_____

_____

Playgroup Pals

NAME:

_____

_____

_____

_____

AGE:

_____

_____

_____

_He who overlooks an offense
promotes good will; he who
repeats a tale separates friends._

—Jewish Proverb

First Organized Play & Learning

NAME OF PROGRAM (AT AGE _____):

_____

TEACHER'S NAME:

_____

FIRST DAY EXPERIENCE:

_____

FAVORITE PART OF THIS EXPERIENCE:

_____

_____

_____

SPECIAL FRIENDS:

_____

_____

_____

Life is about not knowing, having to change, taking the moment and making the most of it without knowing whats going to happen next. —Gilda Radner

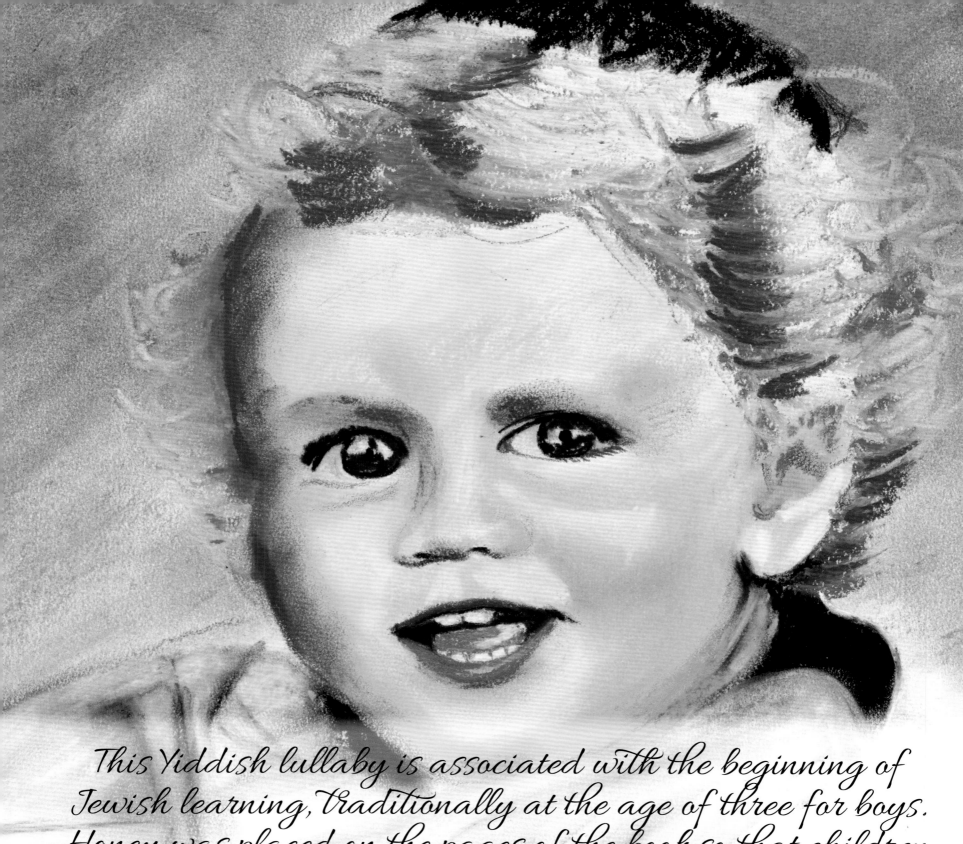

This Yiddish lullaby is associated with the beginning of Jewish learning, traditionally at the age of three for boys. Honey was placed on the pages of the book so that children would associate sweetness with learning.

Oyfen Pripetchick   אויפן פריפעשיק

On the Hearth

Oyfn pripetchick brent a fayerl un in shtub is heys. Un der rebbe lernt kleyne kinderlakh dem alef-beyz.	A fire burns on the hearth and it is warm in the little house. and the rabbi is teaching little children the alphabet.
Gedenkt'zhe, kinderlakh gedenkt'zhe, tayere vos ir lernt do. Zogt'zhe nokhamol un take nokhamol komets alef-o.	Remember, children. Remember, dear little ones, what you learn here. Repeat and repeat yet again kometz alef-o.
Lernt, kinderlakh, hot nit moyre yeder onheyb iz shver. Gliklekh iz der yid vos lernt toyre vos darfn mir nokh mer?	Learn, children. Don't be afraid. Every beginning is hard. Lucky is the Jew who studies Torah. What more do we need?
Az ir vet, kinderlakh, elter vern vet ir aleyn farshteyn vifil in di oysyes lign trern unvifil geveyn.	When, children, you grow up You will understand How many tears lie in these letters and how much crying.
Az ir vet, kinderlakh, dem goles shlepn oygemutshet zayn zolt ir fun di oysyes koyekh shepn- kukt in zey arayn!	When, children carry on the exile You will gain strength from these letters! Look inside them!
Lernt, kinderlakh, mit groys kheyshik, azoy zo ikh aykh on. Ver s'vet beser vun aykh kenen ivri der bakumt a fon.	Learn, children, with enthusiasm As I instruct you. The one who learns Hebrew better Will receive a flag!

Synagogue

NAME OF SYNAGOGUE: **CITY:**

_____

RABBI'S NAME:

_____

CANTOR'S NAME:

_____

FAVORITE PRAYER OR SONG:

_____

FIRST TIME IN SYNAGOGUE (AT AGE _____):

_____

FAVORITE THING ABOUT SYNAGOGUE:

_____

_____

SPECIAL PEOPLE AT SYNAGOGUE:

_____

_____

In Judaism, there are prayers for everything from waking up to eating and drinking to beholding a rainbow! In this way, we are constantly reminded to appreciate all that life presents. What a joyful way to live!

At a family Bar Mitzvah, Beth was at her wit's end with the raucous and uncontrollable behavior of her 5 year old twins, Eli and Aaron.

"Boys!" she whispered sternly, "Do you know why we have to be quiet in the synagogue?"

The boys turned to look at the congregation, and responded, "Because people are sleeping?"

My Child, My Flower

My child is a flower.

Flowers begin as seeds and sprout into the world where they are nourished by two things:

The Sun and Water.

The Sun always knows how to nourish. It always gives just the right amount of light and warmth.

God is the Sun.

But the flower also needs water.

I am the water.

Too much water and the flower will drown. Too little and the flower will die of thirst. I am the wise and gentle rain. I do not over-protect and I do not neglect.

I am the wise and gentle rain.

My flower will grow in the direction of the Sun.

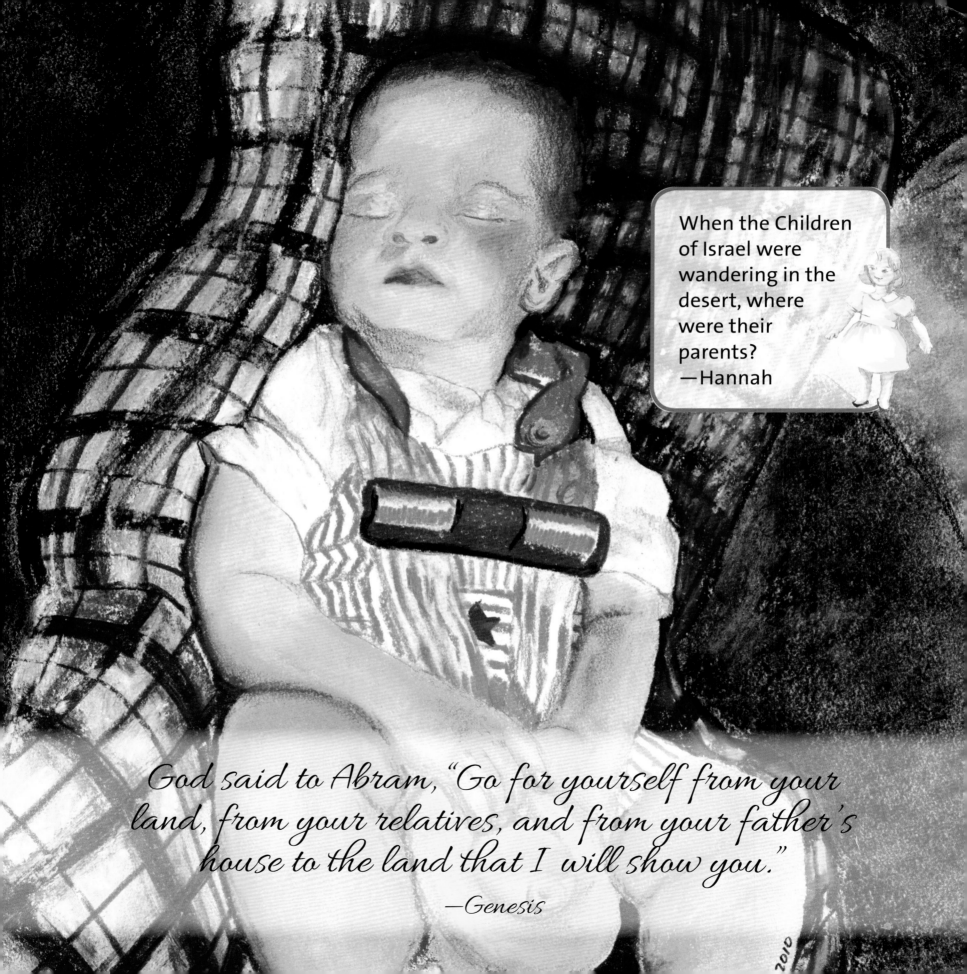

Vacations & Travel

FIRST VACATION BY CAR (AT AGE _____):   DATE

_____   _____

FAVORITE CAR SONGS AND GAMES:

_____

FIRST VACATION BY BOAT (AT AGE _____):   DATE

_____   _____

FIRST VACATION BY AIRPLANE (AT AGE _____):   DATE

_____   _____

OTHER VISITS AND VACATIONS:

_____

_____

_____

_____

_____

Our journey as Jews began with Abraham and continues to this day, scattering us to every continent and to nearly every country on earth. Jewish culture has borrowed and we have given much to the world; most notably, the gift of a moral compass. To be "a light unto the nations" is our commandment and our challenge as we live among them and remain true to our faith.

91

ושננתם לבנך...

You shall teach them diligently to your children... —from the Shema prayer

As the children at Gesher Jewish Day School were learning about the Israelites' receiving the Torah at Mt. Sinai, the teacher asked them to come up with their own Ten Commandments. Josh's was "Do not throw sand in the desert!"

—Josh

Jewish Education

NAME OF SCHOOL:

_____

TEACHER'S NAME:

_____

DATE OF FIRST CLASS:

_____

FIRST DAY EXPERIENCE:

_____

_____

_____

PARENT'S COMMENTS:

_____

_____

FAVORITE PART OF SCHOOL:

_____

_____

SPECIAL FRIENDS:

_____

_____

When Moses was offered the Torah at Mt. Sinai, God asked for collateral before giving something so precious. First the Jewish People offered jewelry, but God answered that the Torah was more precious than jewels. Next, Moses offered our great leaders, but God declined the offer, pointing out that the leaders were already committed to God's word. Finally, the Jewish People offered our children, promising to teach Torah throughout the generations. This, our most precious gift, was acceptable to God & we have been teaching Torah to our children ever since.

—Song of Songs

Train up a child in the way he should go, and even when he is old, he will not depart from it. —Proverbs

Originality is not seen in single words or even in sentences. Originality is the sum total of a man's thinking or his writing.

—Isaac Bashevis Singer

Child's Writing

FIRST SIGNATURE: AGE: DATE:

_____   _____   _____

MORE WRITING: AGE: DATE:

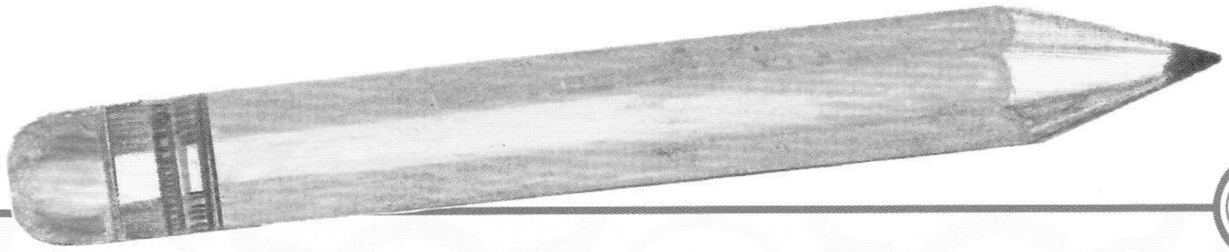

_____   _____   _____

MORE WRITING: AGE: DATE:

_____   _____   _____

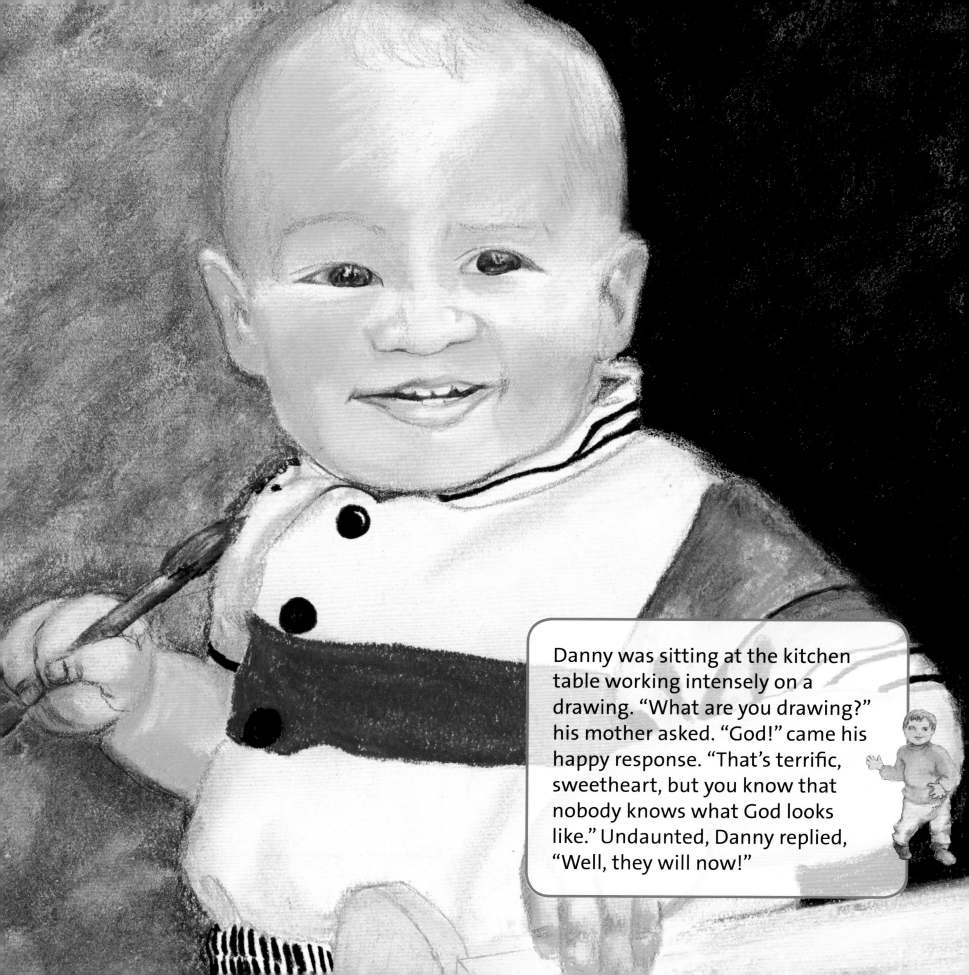

Danny was sitting at the kitchen table working intensely on a drawing. "What are you drawing?" his mother asked. "God!" came his happy response. "That's terrific, sweetheart, but you know that nobody knows what God looks like." Undaunted, Danny replied, "Well, they will now!"

Child's Artwork

AGE: _____   DATE: _____

I have filled him with a Godly spirit, with wisdom, insight and knowledge, and with every craft; to weave designs, to work with gold, silver and copper; stone cutting for setting, and wood carving—to perform every craft. —Exodus

Trust yourself. Create the kind of self that you will be happy to live with all your life. Make the most of yourself by fanning the tiny, inner spark of possibility into flames of achievement.

—Golda Meir

Favorite Activities & Talents

[He] who lives happily does his Creator's will.
—Ba'al Shem Tov

Month by Month 1 to 4

Parents' Reflections

MONTH 1:

_____
_____
_____
_____

MONTH 2:

_____
_____
_____
_____

MONTH 3:

_____
_____
_____
_____

MONTH 4:

_____
_____
_____
_____

HAPPY BIRTHDAY!

We all live with the objective of being happy; our lives are all different and yet the same.
—Anne Frank

Month by Month 5 to 8

Parents' Reflections

MONTH 5:

_____
_____
_____
_____

MONTH 6:

_____
_____
_____
_____

MONTH 7:

_____
_____
_____
_____

MONTH 8:

_____
_____
_____
_____

Days are scrolls,
you may write
thereon only what
you wish to be
remembered.
—Bachya Ibn Pakuda

Month by Month 9 to 12

Parents' Reflections

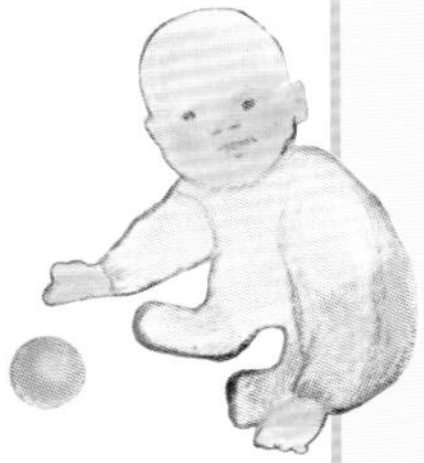

MONTH 9:

MONTH 10:

MONTH 11:

MONTH 12:

ברוך אתה ה' אלקינו מלך העולם
שהחינו וקימנו והגיענו לזמן הזה

Blessed are You, our God, Ruler of the Universe, who has kept
us in life, sustained us and allowed us to reach this occasion.

Happy 1st Birthday

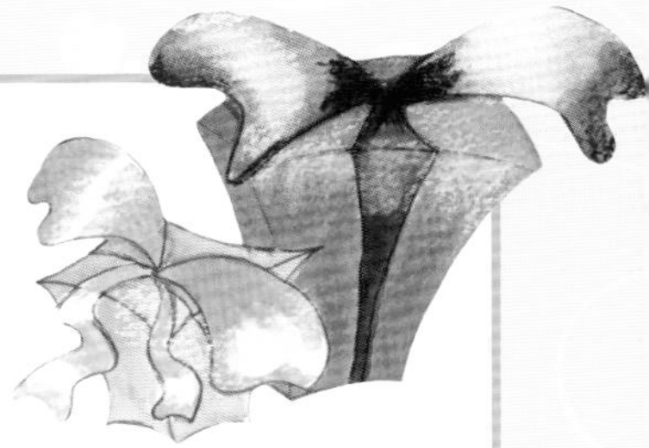

PICTURE FROM FIRST BIRTHDAY

HOW WE CELEBRATED:

_____

_____

_____

PARENTS' REFLECTIONS ON THE YEAR:

_____

_____

_____

_____

Yom Huledet Sameach!

יום הולדת שמח!

..and the years of thy life shall be many.
—Proverbs

Happy 2nd Birthday

PICTURE FROM SECOND BIRTHDAY

HOW WE CELEBRATED:

_____

_____

_____

PARENTS' REFLECTIONS ON THE YEAR:

_____

_____

_____

_____

_____

Yom Huledet Sameach!

יום הולדת שמח!

עד מאה ועשרים

*May you live
to be 120!*

Happy 3rd Birthday

PICTURE FROM THIRD BIRTHDAY

HOW WE CELEBRATED:

_____

_____

_____

PARENTS' REFLECTIONS ON THE YEAR:

_____

_____

_____

_____

_____

Yom Huledet Sameach!

יום הולדת שמח!

בהצלחה!

All the Best!

Happy 4th Birthday

PICTURE FROM FOURTH BIRTHDAY

HOW WE CELEBRATED:

_____

_____

_____

PARENTS' REFLECTIONS ON THE YEAR:

_____

_____

_____

_____

Yom Huledet Sameach!

יום הולדת שמח!

מזל וברכה!

Congratulations
and Blessings!

Happy 5th Birthday

PICTURE FROM FIFTH BIRTHDAY

HOW WE CELEBRATED:

_____

_____

_____

PARENTS' REFLECTIONS ON THE YEAR:

_____

_____

_____

_____

_____

Yom Huledet Sameach!   !יום הולדת שמח

Life Blessing

And in the Book of life, blessing, peace and prosperity, deliverance, consolation and favorable decrees, may we and all Your people the House of Israel be remembered and inscribed before You for a happy life and for peace.

High Holyday Prayerbook

Glossary

ASHKENAZI *literal: German.* Jews of German and Eastern European descent

B'SHA'A TOVA in good time. Common greeting to a woman before the birth of a child

BRIT MILAH covenant of circumcision. ritual circumcision performed on the 8th day of a male child's life

BRIT YITZCHAK *literal: covenant of Yitzchak.* Sephardic custom to welcome a son on the evening preceding the Brit Milah

BUBBE / BUBBIE yiddish name for grandmother

CHANUKAH festival of lights. Eight day holiday commemorating the victory of Judah Macabee over the Syrian-Greek tyrants. The miracle of a small cruze of oil lasting for eight days allowed the Macabees to restore the Temple.

CHANUKIAH menorah. candelabra with nine branches. used on the festival of Chanukah.

ELIJAH ancient prophet. Tradition teaches that Elijah will herald the coming of Messiah. Tradition says that Elijah is present at every Brit Milah (ritual circumcision) and at every Passover seder.

GENESIS first book of the Torah

HAMANTASHEN *literal: Haman cookies.* tri-cornered cookies with fruit filling traditionally eaten on Purim.

HASHEM *literal: The Name.* reference to God

HATIKVAH *literal: The Hope.* Israeli National Anthem

HIGH HOLIDAYS refers to Rosh Hashana, ten days of repentance and Yom Kippur.

KOHEN / COHEN *literal: priest.* member of the Priestly class, a patrilineal descendant of Aaron, brother of Moses. Bat Kohen refers to a woman whose father is a Kohen.

LEVI member of the tribe of Levi, a patrilineal descendant of Moses. Bat Levi refers to a woman whose father is a Levi.

MAZAL TOV *literal: good luck.* usage: congratulations.

MENORAH   candelabrum. Temple menorah has seven branches. Chanukiah, or nine branch menorah, is used on Chanukah.

MIDRASH   *literal: to seek, study or inquire.* explanation or expansion of events of Torah

MITZVAH   *literal: commandment.* usage: good deed

OYFEN PRIPETCHIK   On the Hearth. well known yiddish song traditionally sung on a child's third birthday.

PESACH   Passover. eight day long holiday commemorating the exodus from Egypt.

PIDYON HA BEN   Redemption of the Son. ceremony whereby a first son's obligation to Temple service is symbolically "purchased" from the Kohen (priest)

PURIM   *literal: lots.* festive winter holiday commemorating the triumph of the Jewish People over the evil plot of the king's advisor, Haman. The bravery of the Jewish Queen Esther and her uncle Mordechai are celebrated.

RABBI   *literal: teacher.* spiritual leader

ROSH HASHANA   *literal: head of the year.* new year

ROZINKES MIT MANDLEN   Raisins With Almonds. well known lullaby written by Abraham Goldenfaden (1840-1906)

SABA   hebrew word for grandfather

SABA RABAH   hebrew word for great-grandfather

SAVTA   hebrew word for grandmother

SAVTA RABAH   hebrew word for great-grandmother

SEDER   *literal: order.* refers to the festive meal held on the first (and second in diaspora) evenings of Pesach / Passover.

SEPHARDIC   *literal: Spanish.* Jews of Spanish, Portugese, Middle Eastern and North African descent

SHABBAT (Sephardic pronunciation) / **SHABBOS** (Ashkenazi pronunciation)   Sabbath. day of rest. begins at sundown on Friday and lasts until sundown on Saturday.

SHALOM ZACHOR   *literal: welcoming of the boy.* Ashkenazi custom of welcoming a son on the Friday night after birth

SHAYNA PUNIM   beautiful face

SHOFAR   *literal: ram's horn.* Today the shofar is blown in the synagogue on Rosh Hashana and at the close of Yom Kippur.

SIMCHAT BAT   *literal: happiness of a daughter.* ceremony to welcome a daughter

SUKKAH   *literal: booth.* temporary structure consisting of three sides and a roof through which the sky is visible. used on the holiday of Sukkot.

SUKKOT / SUKKOS   *literal: booths.* festival of booths. eight day holiday commemorating the Israelites' wanderings in the desert for 40 years.

SYNAGOGUE   Jewish house of worship

TALMUD   Rabbinic commentary on the Torah and oral law

TISHREI   Hebrew month in which Rosh Hashana takes place

TORAH   five books of Moses

UPSHERIN   *literal: to cut off.* traditional hair cutting ceremony for a three year old boy.

YIDDISH   language of Ashkenazi origin. Written in the Hebrew alphabet, a fusion of German, Hebrew, Aramaic, Slavic with traces of romance languages. Originated in Germany in the 10th century and spread throughout European Jewish communities.

YOM HA'ATZMA-UT   Israel Independence Day

YOM KIPPUR   Day of Atonement. occurs ten days following the beginning of Rosh Hashana.

ZAIDE / ZAIDY   yiddish name for grandfather

ZEVED HA BAT   *literal: gift of a daughter.* Sephardic custom of welcoming a daughter

Notes

Past and Future

GREAT-GRANDFATHER'S BIRTHPLACE   **YEAR**
_____

OCCUPATION/HOBBIES
_____
_____

SPECIAL QUALITIES
_____
_____

GRANDFATHER'S BIRTHPLACE   **YEAR**
_____

OCCUPATION/HOBBIES
_____
_____

SPECIAL QUALITIES
_____

GREAT- GRANDMOTHER'S BIRTHPLACE   **YEAR**
_____

OCCUPATION/HOBBIES
_____
_____

SPECIAL QUALITIES
_____
_____

FATHER'S BIRTHPLACE   **YEAR**
_____

OCCUPATION/HOBBIES
_____
_____

VALUES FATHER WISHES TO IMBUE IN HIS CHILD
_____

GRANDMOTHER'S BIRTHPLACE   **YEAR**
_____

OCCUPATION/HOBBIES
_____
_____

SPECIAL QUALITIES
_____
_____

GREAT-GRANDFATHER'S BIRTHPLACE   **YEAR**
_____

OCCUPATION/HOBBIES
_____
_____

SPECIAL QUALITIES
_____
_____

GREAT- GRANDMOTHER'S BIRTHPLACE   **YEAR**
_____

OCCUPATION/HOBBIES
_____
_____

SPECIAL QUALITIES
_____
_____

Father's family